Party Blues
By Ismael S Rodriguez Jr

Table of Contents

Dedicated to my fellow veterans and all service members

How to Catch and Miss Your Girlfriend

In each fist, it sits about your neck
That's your "jock" and you wax fucking happy
But there's nothing fun about rape
Or a maim, sort of a toe that's been stop
Or a stunt that ain't fucking worthwhile
You can blink and you'll miss it
But it's within the pantyhose
I saw you by an elm and you were "for real"
You'd had a hero's footsteps that evening
And you recognized your strength
Blushing like cow Perkins ever did
And you smelled sort of
Like a swarthy girl from South Central LA
A fetish pillow with fat mounds of that pink peach
A hooker smell and you told your girl from the pancake
A club that you simply were going bent the garage then
You peeled your head and wrapped your tongue
Up during a lettuce leaf and rolled your head sort of a hockey
Skating team's 2nd rounder during a Walter Johnson Hockey Duel
Then you kissed your girl
And you see yourself cumming within the toilet
Just involved bleach
In the fit, with great care they might smell your body

Home Song

A pair of chopsticks with heels on bent play
Are all four of 'em in prairie grasses, okay?
They smell like hashish, are they?
Looking at a song to me is like
Trying to find a home on the moon
Look at where you are!
I visited a theater with a lover of mine
Dim ridiculous encounter, spurned by that ugly little bitch
What does a man's song mean to a person in a shop for a replacement
watch?
Get new watches and new shoes
Nineteen ninety-nines running down the bridge of a sinking tugboat.
Back to the startling song lamentations urged on a career under the
sway of ignorance
Wear a coma on your head, and shadow-characters will come
To you screaming, even as one would
When the Lord Jesus vomits up a little
So that man that filthy man
That woman smells sort of a tire shredder
He's a gasser, he knows no style
If he was a prostitute, that's all he could throw down
I always hear an album for solace
Have not records and CDs mucking around in my ears
And without a clue on the way to tell what's composed of what
And cast a line on an Island and say what
Who is properly speaking that the narrator for Willy aluminum's
harsh contained claims
Blasting the appeal and notion that masochism, horror, attraction
And therefore, the binaries placed thereon liberation through music's
extension

Bizarre towed behind the music oligarchy's pants enthusiasms
Still relocated to Maya in Colorado's eastern earthen regions
Because no one's heard of them
References of poetry, historically and within contemporary that
followed
Fauves, chanteuses, synths, and poetry
Divisions projected out walls confining and seducing in their
impediments
Indulgences common to musical reverberations of Durham
My antiseptic racial minorities, rap addiction, hip-hop's nihilistic
sociopath
A rabid exemplar of a line in schizophrenic wishes stares us
Within the face and raises the road and rough
For it meets an equivalent line as which its shadow delivers
May be a sense of impending death Calloused rhetoric implanted by
musical monumental
Cannibalizing adventurism no matter who and where he's a gorgeous
oligarch
Well, I assume you should introduce yourself
Check out my books thrill is what I write
So, the next line is Richard on 4th Street

The 80s Eyes

When he finally saw he, she was wearing a mink
The red-and-black beret composes his beady eyes
The temptation was too strong, from the dewy delights of her
Flesh to the deep white delights of her teeth
Dreary, desultory, hypnotic, and soothing
How shall I describe the character of feminism?
Or the erotic aspects of femininity
She may be surly cold and unimpressive
Whispering sort of a mask before the prying eyes of men
"I love you like a bootlegger loves a dead cow"
"I love you like a whore loves a dead man"
"I love you like an amputated penis love a dead penis"
Orwellian in her placards ahead of the Queen
Men cannot only find her sexually appealing
In mouth and eyes and mouth and eyes
Somebody in a park, people on the bridge above
In a lecture a person only to listen to her whisper "I love you"
And she's being ogled, talked about in hushed tones
"it's an accident, female child, nobody likes you here"
Maybe I might have loved her if I'd known
She was fat and ugly, and I'd been gawking at her body
Then would have recognized her as me
Gutierrez would write about the topic of sex and sexual attraction
" Date young women on the side?"
Give me an opportunity, even in our day of celibacy
Everybody girls or boys have their share of affection and desire
And albeit for a time this is not apparent to all or any
You've come to the top of the road for them, in your own
Reproduction and the chits would even have existed on
menrbecker.com

Which, interestingly, was ran from chatbot providers,
demi-billionaires, and mega-hackers
And was a one-man show on a website the domain was .gov
Although check out http://chatswithkeithhaber.org
With various notably rich, nerdy, nerdy rich, nerd, geeks
Who do not have business to be nerd, geeks who run chats with geek
We can change the past
"But internet is geek people, and college graduates from Yale, UC
Berkeley
Even MFA students, some successful entrepreneurs, professionals,
traders
People from bank firm, all nerds—buddy if you ask me"
I've got news for you, men noobs, hamsters, factories
And the INAUDIBLE of web 1.0
All you "men" without wives and youngsters are
Well unless you're in semi-starvation
Just like clockwork, they're suffering, i.e., being replaced
Chocolate chip cookies won't
Not until someone replaces the person who makes them
Sounds like a dream we've all lived.
I mean, this shit ain't new
Yet rather than complaining about how people are replacing them
This shall revolutionize the very structure of human labor

Should Horse

What immortal sculptured thy boldface
Soon shall dark memories recoil
Over rivers, valleys, and rocks?
Never is that the temple of memory
No more his holy mound
With a frowning space or a sigh
So faded was thy brightness!
Who treasured thy jaded brownling
In caverns dank and sepulcher
Deep beneath the tumbled mound?
Those who saw thee of thy days
"By the bed of the river"
Who saw thee crouch and cradle?
A spider, on a northern bank
With its web and crutch
That one, hour, year, and century
Possessed in death and upon the front
Of thy dead form
Ye Puritans met, sir?
'Twas ever thy name in his brow.
I once answered thee it and never went
Although trouble-wrestling stranger
To whose strange bower mine eyes met
And Tewksbury on my lips I won't receive
My first thought, when bosom clung to the breast
Of this tempest-tost. Whispering that, so soon
As the rattle of the clashing boughs faded
To a mutter, poor Indian
Was more adventurer, and cousins
Of Jack Vagante

'Twas but a mile he
Passed, from the woods his wooden-shoed
Redder than the smoke of the coal fire
Of the mill wagon whence such radiance
Shoots his name, white and hideous
So should one not imagine that
I stayed once I heard the decision
Of ill-timed horse called over
The seed of the hidden land
But when suddenly a brush
Must plead for the wary gait
Of its rider, and within
The uplifted hand of his gait
Bowed, I knew the immortal Indian
Was fled and fled
And the white sails of darkness Had stalked
His defiled form and smothered
Its last pulse, bathed within the rising rain
Whoever read described thy dream
Worried by its terrible sage
When idle yet unmourned in
The first age of both
'Twas within the old calendar
By that king of an evil dream

The Girl with Red Hair

You'll concede to your longing
For the soft scent of her and therefore the smell of her
The girl with red hair, the sweetness of a red hair
Climbs the steps, her stilettos smelt of roses
She makes her well beyond middle-aged men
Who plead and wear their furs and robes
Contemptuous of her bent vow
But the girl with red hair will still be the judge
Of her silent disdain, as she walks on
And sweep her fist up the stooping man's back
And throw him into the center of the ground
There the girl with red hair makes it her duty
To cheer up all weary old men,
Spread her red cheeks around their Ching ills
And share within the joy of their hooves and claws
And pushes you down, the breathtaking beauty
That just doesn't melt away
Washes away your cares just like the summer sea
Puts your heart asleep with the girl with long red hair
Lashes out at you time and time again
Your armor breaks and your heart becomes a parable
To miracles, only she will show

The sweetest Girl

All I would like within the world is to love you
The sweetest girl to ever come along
As I climb higher my eyes fill with tears
It seems like the planet was made to be seen
Not one cloud can hide me from you
Go above the clouds and feel the world was made for you
This is the land we were destined for
To give you adequate rain to stay your feet dry
Everything is ideal now
You are the sun, I'm the moon
I'm your lover, you're my sun
We may never be available contact with each other
Is this what we were meant to be?
I won't find a way of peace without you
They've just been made to take a seat and stare
How am I alleged to sleep in this world?
Leave it behind, make a change
They're walking through my nightmares now
Shake it off, get the band back together
Give it all you bought, I'm never returning
It's just a reality when we're growing far apart
I alone I stand beside you
I told you so, so don't stop
Everybody's gone, so can't come
Can't shake this sense, nobody's gonna save me

Why Are You laughing?

Said the small black kitten, "Why are you laughing at me?"
Said the small gray mouse, "Because you're dogs, you're sailors
You sail up the Western Sea
And bite everything they touch
You beat the blue and white polyp peoples
Hard, and eat all they wear"
Said the small yellow dog, "Why are you crying?"
Said the small red wagon, "You are houses and crosses
You are Berbers and Arabs and Turks
And you're frightened at the ocean
You sail on knives in hand
And eat the cedar within the cedar trees
You bring your houses to the water
Slime and therefore the stink of tannin"
And pointed to Ink and Blink and Mustard
And she called them Mud, Moon, Spooks, and Snakes
And said, "You are as bad as all the dogs
You are their phosphoric light
Sunlight, moonlight, or gloom"
And told them to mind their manners
Tea and meat, bread and honey
So, they put their clothes on
And went out into the smelling wind
And they said, "Let's get under the large egg
That has the eggs in it"
And then they went under.
And they settled into the squalling water
For at rock bottom of the egg there have been real ribs and flesh and
bone
And hard things that laid in holes and lay so thick

They had to urge under there to urge out
When they left that place, there was a blue and a squealing wind
Wishing they might stay
But they wanted to travel call at the large blue
Now numerous waters then many beasts
And 1,000,000 miles of dangerous rapids had they to roam
So, they could sleep in peace and be happy
Like the long white house with running water
The white house of singing bells
Now that they had supper, supper was of feathers and buds
And the moonlight was just like the stars out on highways and main
roads
And the birds like crabs during a big pot
And the biscuits were butter and saltwater
Now that they had always a boy at catechism
And so, he had to mention something worth taking note of
Just minutes, words so alike
Now they might sleep within the sun and dream in moonlight
Then the attention of the eagle got very tired
And it took the beetles or some little tree
And put them in water and planted them in it
So, when the rabbit required a breath of fresh air
Or something to eat
The birds would come and sleep in the lake and obtain out a cup
Now their hearts beat so quick that they had to run on top of the sun
Or lie on mud, before they might be courageous
Being thought of so artlessly by men
Now in the dark, the birds would lie on the bottom
And tell themselves they're the gods
And bend to form a tree substitute autumn strong
Then they might attend sleep by the shell or on sticks
Weep afterward by the sole window, that they might find

Then the hearth shivered and melted into the snow
And the wind laughed and therefore the little wide lips laughed
Now in Europe, they need birds which will break
A glass and blow a whistle at you, good luck
Now they send a mentor to sell the sun
And say it won't be up goodbye
But now you're coming and bringing back your brothers
With your lashings like that broomstick
And swinging your face is all swollen up
In a moment you ought to all say, "I go"

The Story of the Dragon Sea Lion

He was a true and truly the dragon tried to harm her
And eventually knocked her right out when she was asleep
Now the very thoughtful little black kitten that lived together with
her
She called her Kitty and she said don't hurt me!
I'm a true animal a bit like her, yeah
We had big black rabbits and chickens and rats
And we had this tiny white cow, and she called her Jack
He was so little, and when he was young, he was brave, big, and
powerful
And really opened over the water for boys to the boat
He loved the water and fishing and fishing brought us frozen dessert
And once we visited the church the small black mouse called her Ruth
And she was always picking strawberries for welcome tea
I and she loved to travel rowing and that I looked out the window of
the boat
And I saw the small white cow running by, and that they became good
friends
And then Kitty came out with Ruth and she said don't hurt me!
I'm just a true cow a bit like her
We had granny cows, blue ribbons, big white ribs
Big white steaks, goats, and therefore the two little ones back-to-back
I'm not like your cows; I'm not beef or lamb
And why am I called a cow?
I'm just the thing like an old southern cow
I just sorta appear as if one!
Now I loved to bake, and I loved to eat
And I loved school
Now the opposite dog killed Donkey
It was twins

I've always been very quiet
And this is often how I didn't wanna be known
I haven't moved since then
I think about the fisher and therefore the white kitten and the little
grey mouse
And all the fun times I had with my pigs and that I remember
I wonder why I do not remember that
When I was five, please don't kill me
Also, it tells about the dress that I wore once I was a touched girl
So, I do not know what it says, but I do know the sensation I had once
I saw it
It's me that day and that time, you know
He Loves You because you were his little moon
He loved you because you so seemed like the moon
You couldn't be his little moon
Or he'd be angry and throw you down
Or he'd break you into little pieces
And he'd have fun with you
And he loved you because you were a dragon sea lion
He looked down at you and he loved you with a baby
And you didn't know you were a dragon sea lion
And that's why he loves you now, you know
In misty blue seas, he trains you
And until you're ready for sea, you know
He'll love you till you're ready for sea

The Beat

The beat was throbbing in her vertebrae
The splinter from a screw slipping through her skin
The strange wholeness of the courtyard
She sinks her thumb into my thigh
Closing her eyes in ecstasy
Her skin tinged with red, blood surcharged
Pursued confusion and dared defiance
Delirium as did she, then he was gone
A vision of limbs long lost legs
Darkly misaligned, jaws, loose neck
Thoughts of his flesh
She sat for a long time in her orgone
Frightened, I rested the index
At the window and closed it closed
Multiple valleys of bullshit
White horseshoe of hurricanes obscured
In the dream a cluster's stench saturated the air
Minutes I stood in front of her with Dixie cups
I wished I had air for seconds of trance
The orchid was the opposite
Vanished, leaving the apple-green sky
Orange-tipped raindrops, I swayed, broke
"Nervous?" Fucking impossible
"Please don't make the mistake we made" I said
My girl nearly alive, blood rain down, helping another
Merging in the perpetual side effects of ketamine
I led her back to the counter
Three tones, don't have to be come, peel, grab the plunger, then pull
There was a sound, an explosion
The signal inside her brain had gurgled, pumped up with pressure

"Your heart tingled at the sign of doom," I said
"And with a jackhammer" she was dead. "No?"
"I'm supposed to shut up"
I ran the plunger
Cough syrup in her mouth, the jagged hinge of her neck
Seeping black holes, doing to her a slow death, lips kinked
We stood in the dusty parking lot of the motel
Two watches, faintly beeping
Five semesters in the city forever meant stamina
The time away from our bodies leaked into our dreams
Where it overlaid and coincided with the time in our heads
When the lovely girl we sometimes called her "Alice"
Wept on the pavement beside us was still
Lay there, felt the exterior of her skin change
Over the six fractional minutes basically just before she died
I knew the feeling, twine around my heart
Jostling me out of home, like a stray cat in a suite of high-rise condos
Then a tape recorder started whispering to me in my ear
"The only thing you've ever loved is suffering
Every friend you've ever made is a lie
You're dead?
Who's telling you these lies, and with you, whom do you love?
The radio had the story first
She's been smoking crack for hours
With a dead guy in the passenger seat
I still can't forget how you look to me now
Like you did when we met
In a dark room on some cheap motel floor
"I'm so proud of you, I don't know what to do"
His English was a mess
"Talk to me, go home, I'm going to the dealer"
Tonight, two performers trying to be a part of them

I looked at her face, a face I hope I never see again
Sweat erupting under her ring
"We're so ashamed It's been so long since
We got together that we can't understand do you know?"
Looking at her for a long time
"No"
Stuttering I'd hurt her that much
"Who's this name I hear they ask you at the end?"
"Mommy"
"Oh, come on, it's been so long and it's only—"
"All moderns, I know. Without your memories of our life together
I won't know what to believe. I mean, fucking tragedy
Why the fuck did you have to die like that?"
The dog's barked and the trash men came together
She's wet and messed up
"We can't believe you're still hanging around in an abandoned house
With booze around and look in anything, man's hand
fucking your face and lips you don't even remember her
How you were thinking they got in a clear head when I pulled her
dress...
What's done well with me tomorrow

The Secret Temple

Inside this secret temple
I cast innocence's reminder of ocean blue
Her open hands wrapped around my waist
We were both shy and silent
As she took my goddess thrust in her mouth
The beautiful taste of her snow-white skin
I could feel my soul just flowing into her
I wandered away to undertake recreating my reverie in my room
I rushed myself with a straightforward and innocent mantra
A crystal mirrored room and that I received that pink and white night
Lights were neon during this temple
And that I associated with those little golden lights
The room was a door that led to an excellent white plain
All my senses were consonant as I eroded to Greece

Who's Message?

If I'm to be as honest as I am fair
She looks at the planet for what it's clothed to be
A beautiful girl with a tragic past
I remember the way she refused to face some challenges
But like her, I'm a person during a world
That's crammed with many difficulties
Love isn't an endless dungeon
Where every floor may be a different color
I love the labyrinthine theory, now the most force
That simply captivates me with the treasure
But nothing creates the waypoint
It produces feelings of joy
When I'm alone in my front room
Sitting ahead of the TV
The color red infuses those colors
It's true love's fleeting and leaves no satisfaction
A mixed haberdashery filled with
Wannabes, ambitions, hoodlums, and terrorists
I last walked that road once
Once I worked at a taxi agency
I packed my bags as speedily as an American smoker
And right once I arrived home, I started to smoke
The increase in nicotine caused me to fall
Becoming monosyllabic like an elderly person
The will to escape from the busy city streets
They say there's nothing more useful than the phone
That should be the safest place to be
In the middle of a crowd!
It isn't a handset; it is a telephone box!
Downtown Houston within

The late afternoon of the second week of June
Where the air conditioner
Was making me consider the horror of Europe
I must not lose this amount of speed
It is difficult to stay going when the stop has become
That smaller than the compartment
During which I park at a flower shop
But the smile thereon handsome face
Is within the peculiar situation as if he's thinking
About a redhead, he saw casually admiring a tree...
But right after a car, he casually stopped his car
And sat by that very friend who taught him everything he knows
Everything he knows I will be able to make
The excerpt for you to require this quiz
I desire bending my head and searching up into that face
Sitting next to me. Her telephone shining bright
And she's having fun doing something
She moved the pieces within the air
Right after I pressed the stop button
She used her phone to call her friend
In my opinion, that is the biggest reason why I see enduring
Sketches together of the best sorts of art
Of course, it isn't exactly what it's like if you look closer
But the middle and corners are so alive and vivid
There's a fantastic liveliness that can't be explained
A sense of connection, the engine-like urge for the work to continue
I remember a gorgeous girl who embodies all the power
To get on the great and high side and to let her guard down during a
way
Who's calm when right after midnight she starts singing to herself

Fantasy Where I Even Have Never Been

I have this fantasy where I even have never
Had to travel back due to graduate school
I have this fantasy where it's okay if I forget to eat
Because I even have never let myself get hungry
I have this fantasy where the main target
Isn't on me but on the work, I'm doing
I have this fantasy where I even haven't ever noticed how old my scar is
I have this fantasy where I even have never betrayed my friends
I have this fantasy where I even have never had to figure for my life
I have this fantasy where people think I'm crazy
Because I do know what it's to be frightened of being dead
I have this fantasy where everyone will say they support me for making
this decision
I have this fantasy where I can anticipate to writing
About my world from now forward and not worry about any sort of
judgment
I have this fantasy where nobody will judge my confidence or my
ability to handle my weight
I have this fantasy where I will be able to never need
To see what I feel is that the dirty secret that killed some people
I have this fantasy where everyone will know my power
I have this fantasy where there's an open door
And that I can become a pacesetter for my community because I even
have never left
I have this fantasy where my body is safe from abuse
And that I could walk the fine line between self-care and nutritional
necessities
I have this fantasy where I'm already doing all the tutorial preparation
that I want
I have this fantasy where I never awaken battle-weary

From the day I walked amidst the dead and dying
I have this fantasy where nobody has ever been mad at me
For saying on camera that I used to be glad that each one of this was
happening
I have this fantasy where nobody has ever told me I appear as if I'm a
fucking loser
I have this fantasy where I never felt comfortable during a room of
white men
I have this fantasy where I'm enough of a professional MFA candidate
That I can walk into the MFA programs throughout NYC and be a
success
I have this fantasy where I'm a walking literary resume
I have this fantasy where I do not need to be attractive for anyone
I have this fantasy where I can solve
All of the world's problems because I would like to

Survival Lyrics

You have contemplated the woods
And therefore, the skies
And they are sure not to be seen
For their thorns and prickles
They are mock mountains turning green
And weeping bright-eyed dewdrops
That raindrops within their wheat coats
Are watering the almost-starving grasses
Not my fairy tales
It is pure ingenuity
Which reminds me
Of an excellent idea
For a survival album
I for my part only clank
On the bell-ringing brachiosaurs
For the giants now
Down below me seem feeble
Somewhat hopped up I'll confess
Then I used to be any time last week
Their voices are in unison now
Very dear and sweet without a sorrow
And they inquire from me whether I do know
How they're keeping the snow
As I even have heard within the plaintive yelps
Walking amongst the slopes
Taking an in-depth look
Would are an exquisitely gallant thing
However perhaps a mentor
Would have let it continue for 100 years
These are the rocks that are beneath me

Let me allow them to speak in direct words
To the silent giants and to me
Let me see them as they stand
Their heads down gazing up into the heavens
And I hold in my hands a book
Hope, hope, for a world lost
Shall not be lost alongside me

The Art of Losing

The wife who loved me
And her two daughters
Had gone into exile
The art of losing isn't hard to master
I lost my beloved poacher
But as friendship fades thick
The very fingers that longed to relish his attack
Delivered to mate
He was mischievous
To require his place
The art of losing isn't hard to master
I lost a book I'd picked up within the streets
From a bookseller leaving them within the shelf
But to tarry, to order a second copy
To read in my office and thrift
Another for my time-traveler
And keep the third empty
None of those will bring disaster
The deaths of life-mates
What a surprise
When I'd feared the danger of change
Death in marriage, death in life
What a shock
The loss, losing to relationship
Once I knew I should
Have loved my sibling Gianna
Who died amid excellent
The death of siblings the nation's belated triumph
And because of the assassin who wasn't extinguished
My rivalry to Gianna

The death of a beloved artisan
It's going to seem trivial
Other complacent and benign slanders
Such as the loss of a family way finder
As I parent by telephone, but I remember
Loudly, that the kid is mid-bypassed by cancer
And at the mercy of the advisers
By those that outbreed
And as therein family as in my very own
I've lost Bianca and Leonardo an excellent artist
I lovable, I like, I wanted that. But then, later, slightly
I lunched with my good friends from the community
In the age of radio, just before tragedy happened
Let's out of love.
My sister, Ellie who lived with a little brother I loved
A tenacious man, a powerful man, an area policeman
Expecting the life his son couldn't take him
The love of damned exile, killing love
What a shock, the loss of Ellie Bianca and Coleman
At the trusted clutches of both Good Neighbors
My son's friends, then the slim ease
With my dear friend Dick, his friend, one among the guard
Thirteenth this century
It's dangerous to practice during a Field of Past Tasks
Because people will encounter
I've six children, a boy, a girl, and a woman
The loss of boys and girls the painful ones,
The ones who withered within the cold
The loss of friends
The loss of family relatives
Who far they get only by natural
Or not uncommon circumstances

Am departing, only coming hither, on their answer
The wars, so few which sometimes there'd be one
On every corner, and American, European
And then one literally directly on a window
Like cops interviewing an event, the way that sometimes
Complex and funny things, equally human...
And the landing. But all firm, the feet without error
The deaths of friends and intimates
All men and ladies
I love! Our hearts quiver for everyone
The compulsion to loose on them
To ascertain them returning here
My Uprising voice the pain left hanging on
The camp wall it's extremely vivid
The lover who vanished
And didn't come then disappeared from my Intuition?
I remember where I came from T
he very fact that the crowds were processing starboard
Looking down by time because it passed each hour
Loaded with life the signaling, the tackle-backings
And teardrop-casings to shake the water
Beautiful birthdays
The deaths of birthday guests, all alone, frisking at the door
The crossing of the edge the pain
The pain turned petty, in order that mine
Everything would empty into sunlight
We'd float out again and really slowly
The party exploded up through the footlights
I heard my friend Leandro
What was happening within the kitchen
Buti do not remember
I heard a cello in his room: I work too

He heard my brother shout
I'll see some sound

Fall Diversity

For the autumn of all worlds
He's forever
We must not give discretion
To the winds of charge
Do not fall to shape and value
When you won't see them in the least
And once more the pearl
He sticks out of his ear and he steers away.
A supper of diversity without sacrifice
Planting seeds of her tribe's crop
Plants round her weed's curtains, birdseed
Plants and trees don't mock human beings
Trees lead people, and mountains
Are the wind that carries them along hills
Preferring not to starch but water
Rich but forest thin
Sweets thin they are
Thick seed they are walkers
Wreckers, healers, rejecters of all things
Are the breadth of the river
And swift canoers
Just as we are along the slough of battle
In the boughs of the trees
We are sons of angels
And within the branches of cave redwoods
We stand at rock bottom of moments
Preceded by women
With the heavy axes derisive of men
Rejecters, Nulls and Turner's Take
The boughs of our trees

Perish on the sides of traffic;
The fells of our mountains
Touched by men
One might see the river rise
One may have a glimpse of the wind
United we stand as we've managed to face
Not alone against the sharp fringe of a pencil
But alongside of an incredible thick faith
Let us redo the way we dream
Our dreams are aimed after others
Though others' dreams have transformed us
We are absorbing
I couldn't inscribe
How it's going to be
An awakening
Behind this ripple
In which there'll be stories
Blithe the shared flows
And eternities
Along the wave
Until then, Earth Mover
Like rush before freeze
Afoot the longer term can't be had
"Hey there, bitch," shrieks a person
At his flatbed truck
Who is refining his small wheels on the bridge
Above Summerland's bluffs
He's an Armadillo
The guy... he's...
He's smart as hell.
Upside down on the ottoman
The Natives from the Inland Coast

The last of the gritty surf bastards

The Grand Engine

And in the full and solitary evening
Upon a planet of heavenly beauty shine
The flowers, the birds, and of all the skies
The blooming sunbeds and the whiter stars
Shining like radiant gems in the orb of heaven!
Comrade, these last scenes of the drama,
Which occupy the remainder of my time,
Have, ere we're through, taken their way back
Through my heart to me, like light and joyous glories
Thro' the clash and valor of patriotic fame,
Drowning out all the blood and tears of those
Whose high luck and wisest counsels have this day
Avail'd against the blood of a part of their countrymen
They have carried my heart up from the darksome cells
Of this accursed ghetto to daylight, in dreams
Of all the exultant revolutionary scenes
Of your admirable progressive, advanced state
And now it doth draw me to devote all my powers
To your refined and sublime form of government.
Entering the city, near the temple of the
"Power and Law of God" the fiery bridge now
And dwelling-place of the fortitude and courage of me
A dreary, tedious dungeon was find'd ready
Where I was lodged, call'd by the gaoler's feet
Or trussed by the ragged rags by shades
But I am not to be denied, or suffered to indulge
My fondest dreams of liberty! Whither are you flown?
And what purpose have you sent me to this place
Of imprisonment and exile?
This ill-fated and miserable spot is not a

Never-land, where love and sisterhood maxims
Endurable in this resort will be forever blotted out by
Tyranny and prejudice, nor is it our liberty
Which must make its final and lasting station here
I shall do no more than pity this travesty
And thou know'st no law restraining our anger
Ere our stern virtue make a triumphant entrance
He shews not a gentleman's humility, but scorns
With degrading looks all the virtues of the good
Who love him, and who lie under his generous handling
Queer Princes women they are, beguiling and effeminate
Who declare to us, that my lady loves her lover even
As I do my own sisters; the mothers mock me with
This hypocritical similitude, who declare
That my gentle mistress loves me as her own daughter.
Thus, the Grand Napoleon refuseeth, as we are importunate
To make his cause and that of his country brought
To the tribunal of the supreme judges of the
World, in this lower domain of these dark places
Where his powerless power lies prostrate, yet fears to die
Behold the daub'd engine of Tolstoy's "God of Carnage"
In the fiercest rage or passion; and this engine
Stirreth sometime to the thundering howl
But spasmodically systematically happy is he, and inspires
O'er the persons that he has most terrify'd,
With fearless, implacable scorn, as if all his people
Were of human form, as this device is, but like an organism
Of such a nature, that is, they are doing the trope
When to them a fresh or overrflood
Or then with a fierce mielie, blasts the plot
And through a shriek and to the Russian roar
Of Selim's mighty sword and the care of Louis' throne

This modern work of impending destruction sped
Yet the storm's wash'd and wove like a spider-web
Till the ancient original, unshackling at great cost
Alleviate those that were the most incurable
Passing this dreadful place, and greeting one
Who apparently air'd some great importance
I found the name much misspoken; for Putin
Having been a pupil of the master and disciple
Of Tolstoy, master of carnage and the happiness of
More miserable than those who feel themselves
With him!

My Journey to My Life

I've failed in my duties
I've failed in my mother's will
I've failed in my town's laws of hospitality
I have disgraced my father and mother's memory
I've failed in my duties to my company
I've failed in my duties to my country
I've failed in my duties to my lord
In pledging my life for his honor and country
I've failed in my duties to my enemies
I've failed in my duties to my wife
My mother's dying breath against me
And my country marked by the good stain
Such is my responsibility, for I count not my years
I've failed in my duties.
I've beaten an old man during a duel
I've disgraced my very own name and noble lineage
I've embarrassed one among my very own brothers
And I am casting my lot in with someone second
I have failed in my duties to my company
Under my command my Knights dwell dying and dying
My Knights are going to be with me have I died today
I've beaten an enemy to death to not live longer.
I've killed a Sister of Mercy
I have betrayed an ally at the value of my life
I've blamed a foe for my failures of life
I haven't done anything to earn my service anymore
I've failed in my duties to my Lord
My Lord mourns on behalf of me, and my mother has nothing to
mention
I am undeserving of an honorable burial

And if I die, I will be able to attend the grave with the remainder
I have failed in my duties to my country
My brother's brother, the King of Lombardy
Has commissioned me for killing a spear-point within the leg
He is greater than my father and that I can pay for this
I have committed treason, my Lord will know this
The way it's written I even have failed in my duties
I have dishonored my lands thanks to my drunken carelessness
And in my nightmares my dead brothers call me names

The fourth of the Man's

The consecration of man's spirit
Would call forth the holy, and be duly
Woven into a replacement ballad
Rise, ye thinkèd heroes, and again the visions
Will give recall to all or any your thoughts
Then arise, O champions, for cruel death
Hath suffered all of you. Whoso all's
Sabre, and cutlass, delights and brown swearers
Now all arm'd with swords or fireballs
Of swaggering despisers and like bold boys
To engage the death-plays of death
Whose wars're ardour'd afresh by the abominable
Compare, this opportunity have brought you to the present place
And hold you warred against 'tis all
Warring, hasten, for war's the drama of life
Weep not for the lady you're keen on so dearly
Doom'd to the harlot, for they've killed each other
Brav'd your hearts this woeful security goodbye
And yet now you stand our momentous choice
And ere goodbye have lovers beget wearies
Of true sorrows goodbye giant heavy
Th' unequal night tasks us anew and draws us
To storms and deep seas, in order that all
Of us by his private thoughts slays; who then
Shall be left for ever to measure and end
As mist or smoke, or as man or bird, or some decaying tree
He is long gone, give us lightrope, and for a sign
That shall quickly reach your chars, invoke the fourth
Phantom Sweep. Take deadly aim. Guard your own Sword
From their step they swiftly approach; few four folks dare

To fight from six thousand swords. With many a terrible oath
Leave not one empty-handed from the axe-head
And pierce off one among the four biggest heads together with your
Sword
Whom ye slay make certain, together with his pity ye pervert
Tremendous sorrows to miserable woe and woe
You teach your children to render

The Fire That Burns

You have trouble thinking
Who am I
The fire that burns
Cuts out your initials
And makes your name
Unpronounceable
The gas that burns
Cuts out your favorite songs
You sing to yourself
You wish for yourself
While everyone else
Won't understand.
That's why I cover
My paper once I read
The words I wish to write down
I wish to understand
If we do not know
What the words mean
Like me, you look below
And above
Some people mention you
Like it's nothing in the least
It is like, everyone knows
That you are something
That you are something,
If you'd only move

Summer Shore

More alive than always
One among his beasts of burden
Can precede him within the checkpoint
Once the ascetics of the shore at the check point
He loses the bird across the park to the killers
Isolated point within the shadows
Ten o'clock within the night
Its imprint on the stone
It's a sublime urge
To climb up off the bottom
And reach out your hand!
It is a primal urge, a desire to fly
Above stoat, above the dawning sky,
To start but to fall, be alone
Like a leaf within the fall
He's dog counted mice
Critically wounded after each attack
The checkpoints ping, long-distance Washerwomen
Birds of prey converge and therefore the humans fall
A lethal panther and a mortal cub
Tackled simultaneously
Because the tranquil river runs into its rising flood
And imperceptible paws pull the beasts out of the water
With equally uneventful swims
Time grows pressing. Jet one, we'll leave
He is lost within the expansive sea and swim
Far from Aranoch. the world won't collapse
Like tidal waves to observe a hero's final pursuits
He has fallen twice, first within the schooner
That separated two aspects of his mind

Once water and twice the land
But now his reason and body are just like the open sea
Libya is an orbit above the substance
He is the veteran and therefore the newest engineer
And each event they need to make to survive builds the narrative
Together, throw one, show him, promise to consult
Eating cactus and stars, the mountain is named the Maker's star
To cross is to cross over the blade
Each rig the son of heaven whose life went on here
Every false dawn each here, each here,
Each boost sure of the promise of success
We've forgotten the knot and therefore
The faithful eye on the cherished bird
Then you've got to shop for the ticket four years brings no more tickets
The reader knows my "how"
The page is empty there's no preamble
To outline a riddle that plagues us both
That is persistent, that's exhausting
that imparts a sturdiness to our meetings
It won't open as this profound paradox has undone time's stitches
Where was this half oblique confidence, what was it about?
Even the neighbor said yes, as he devotes six years of his life
To a crumbling grace
And the first time I meet him nine years ago
His speech has a metaphorical tenacity
He's a mixture of cynicism, child, art spotter, music promoter
So last summer, he showed me the video
The "feeble and reflective women"
Who encircle the streets because the cruise ship cruises
Their eyelids are closed
They're crowded on narrow conical poles, guiding the lads
Diplomacy, embarrassment, peacekeeping

Truly void?
The questions repeat sort of a spent string of baroque flourishes
He is laughing, his lips are blue,
It is hard to create within him an area
I make the observation
He motions at the conclusions on his countenance
and looks uncomprehending
The mirrors and messianic imagery take you away
He is reading softer, and he plans words

The Death Story

The gods cannot rage against us
As the events during this tale have proven
Too many of us died over an easy question
These are the ways in which
All are strangers to at least one another
So slowly, their laughter eventually fails
And even as my client realized
It had been probably for the simplest
No scream left unaddressed...
The intimate pictures taken and their stories
Were shared with the various
Who took part during this performative
The death story inside it all...
We gathered at the rear of the cafeteria for the wake
Though local gossip surrounded her
A woman like her appeared to prefer mobbing me
The tables near me were reserved
And therefore, the flow of individuals seemed stifling
Then, one by one, the guests began to scroll through their Quills
They might still be ready to raise images within the present
But the memories were far beyond what one could comprehend
Everything was screaming to urge out

Happiness Imagination

I am the laughter of the Waves
I am the living soul of the river flowing past
I am the sunshine of the morning light
I am the caress of the morning breeze
I am the urge of the daystar
I am a sweet voice of the northern star
I am the strength of the morning sun
I am the memory that dwells
Within the hearts of these that knew me
I am the shadow that dances on the edge of your vision
I am the wild goose that flies south
At autumns call and that I shall return at Summer rising
I am the gentle rain that falls upon your face
I am the spring flower that pushes through the dark earth
I am the chuckling laughter of the mountain stream
Do not weep on behalf of me for I even have not gone
I am the memory that dwells within the hearts of these that knew me
I advance with an important heart
I am the wind that shakes the mighty Oak,
I am a sleigh pulled by four mistresses
I am the day that is too frosty
I am the snoops gathered to observe us
I am the sailor on a ship pursued by a ship's lantern
I even have a belly sort of a snake.
I am the life that is waiting within the soil
To supply two plants which will come forth and plant their seeds
I am the wind that shakes the mighty Oak
I am a sage with eyes of gold and shilling silver
I am the day that has no name
I am the khabs that shine in my face

I am a man with a sickle in my hand that breaks red corn
I am the mourning ivory in his clothes
I am the autumn wind that drifts over ground
And plays with the waves here and there
I am the woods and therefore the birds that sing to me
I am the crows on the horizon
I am the red stone that wears the tears of roses
I am the story of the twofold old man who likes spring
I am the rusty catch within the crook tied to the stone pillar

The Girl with a Tattoo

Now she's long ago gone
Going home for the day
The girl with a tattoo
Shit happened in her life
Whose child, was she?
The girl with a tattoo
Oh! Her name was Lily
She was an extended way from home
She was so beautiful
The girl with a tattoo
Oh! Fretta had what
Had what she wanted love
What? what percentage years she'd been alive
The girl with a tattoo
You were so hot
Oh, is she dead?
She was a touch fly
Her knickers were down
The girl with a tattoo
Oh! Her name was Denial
She was getting to Miami
She was living the dream pretending its true
And she was still alive
Oh! She loved her parents
That Mama and Papa wouldn't go
She was just meek
The girl with a tattoo
Oh! The boys all liked her
She had sexy hair and an enquiry history
She was happy, she was hot

The girl with a tattoo
The kids were everywhere her
Her big tits got tons of men
Her fingernails were surreal
The girl with a tattoo
Oh! The boys wanted her
She was cute and fat
She was so fun
The girl with a tattoo
The homophobia is past now
Her story is soon to be told
And she'll be a size 0 just like the rest
The girl with a tattoo
Oh! Now your old coppers
Are bringing her home
Maybe the police will act
She will be no more
You are all responsible
The girl with a tattoo
Oh! it is the truth a method or another
The girl with a tattoo
Oh! Her name was Memory
She was an honest girl
The girl with a tattoo
Oh! Her name was Anna
She was the boss of the house
She won't walk behind me
And sing Bela Lugosi's Dead
The girl with a tattoo
She's gone
She's gone
Holy shit

Torment Ecstasy Chocolate

But if we could share this together, then no worries together with her
in you
All could be well for her your Nina and Shannon
What are you trying to find torment during this delightful body?
Whichever you discover, could also be a meager number of erogenous
nerves
Or a high confine your gaping lips, gently sucking
To find the recipe for this babe's ecstasy you will have to long to fuck
Come as several specimens are sealed away, let me strain for you now
She's only a delicacy to strip this soul once it's well done
When you wear her and luxuriate in her you'll seduce just like the
purple one
Or the don't-know-your-number-how-on-tte
What am I able to say, never mind
This is the type of fetish she'll pull from her hot, wet, harem. Sorry
Chocolate iced tea with a touch of that when prized, always pricy
Licking her lips are might to shiver in anticipation
You'll fall to your knees for hands but keep nice and well clothed on
her
Shots of cold champagne looks pretty once we sip it
Glass drops quickly when it hits this delicate skin, I'll drink you...
That would be perfectly fitting to mention she's a shy ahhh sweetheart
I prefer this intimate moment once we reach that degree of intimacy
Her heart-symbol I'm sure we'll go down all night
Can feel and luxuriate in the friction of her body the way you've never
known
Seen with a pinhole or bestowing every mouthful
One slick tongue for you to nibble on her teeth with lust
The he's left confused with the scenes beyond

He does know to be limber to be the previous couple of swears he'll
dare say
And is so strong and filled with our hips that we cannot let her go
So, show him this body altogether it's fine delicacy
Let us take her completely against our will
We shall be having all types of surreal, or pornographic fantasies
And get completely lost by this example where our desire is claimed
Not even once can we suppress the powers and excitement of our loins
We're crazy, but neither half that crazy man nor speak with a word
Support fights for focus or control the mouths of us from inside all the
way
Speak for yourself she reaches the toughest part
Appearing to be straight from the shower, I need to know why...
To clean all of her rays...
This is your tongue on her soft flushed cheek
If I do not find your tongue symbiont to an act of affection
Please be my slave I'll down ration coffee or chocolate at bad as each
day
I look after your callous gone bad taste on my throat...
I swore tons of pills until I quit but got no relief...
Gasping into her hand, I sit on a chair and wink a demon thus far
Looks like I'm teasing today for your taste or want also

Romance America

I discuss the major events of the day with you
"Today may I tell you a little story" she says
And I give her the details
And it is a story of the long-distance relationship
Of the million plus words we wrote
Of the exact date we were promised
That we would meet at a time to be determined
By the very optimistic driving directions drawn on a clipboard
And of the torturous existence of a stream of phone calls
Every time the world shifted, and I looked the other way
She says of our fortunes that leaving hasn't been easy
But I have had my fill of long-distance love
To be in love with someone who isn't physically near is
Terrifying, but even though I know that I only have hours left
I still feel the urge to call every day
So, is there anyone here who hates long distance?
There sure are, but I feel like things are better here
Why?
Because the running water's stocked
Says the sign, and I can paw through the bins if it's starting to get late
Isn't America great?
A question that I would ask whatever country this was
But in my head, I hear this kind of whine:
"I find the struggles of push and pull
Mistake and fall, repose and enjoyment
Exceptions and expectations
Discipleship and dissension
Heresy and dogma
Good and evil
sink or swim

Find balance in the struggle"
Another reason my delusions weren't spreading
Was because my diagnosis included paranoid schizophrenia
As well as schizoaffective disorder
And every time I tried to treat with antipsychotics
I relapsed, and then had to start over again
With a new batch of prescription medications
So now, I am listed on the waiting list for both
If you used to talk to me all day long
what would you say back?
A picture would form in my mind
Altered by an ad campaign
And when I was lost, in a forest
There was always a forest just around the corner
and I would run past it
somewhere, far, far away
I am not lost!
I'm running!
Never more and never less
Running after the tomorrow that never comes
Running after tomorrow's promises
For it is tomorrow that is in my brain
Trying to find it in its endless vagueness
And because I am a mirrored image
I often did not know I was torturing myself with words
So, is it any wonder I fail
Maybe I can't write romance novels anymore
I guess I can't write just plain songs
But I'm writing four volumes of poetry by now
With a nonfiction collection coming once the dust has dried
To the cynical, these might all look like victories
But I've learned not to worry

Because I've always been the optimist
And I do believe that what I've come to learn
Is that there are times to still be mad and peppy

Chakra Innovation

Kether absorbing all notions, both present and past
Disaster, innovation, development, all are connected with Kether
Even light itself, the nature of Light, is derived from the pondering of
Kether
Nothingness is fluid, gleaming and alive, explode-able musical notes
Not contained by tarot cards
Chakra hydration
Fermented illusions of Kether
Breast cancer being checked by the shapeshifting mirror and tattoos
Ripping on a razor blade wrapped around a wad of sins
The people living like ghosts, upside down, thick wraiths
A sword whispering to its master, a shining angel guiding you to one
The where, the what and the when
Is not important because all things are connected.
Kether only exists to manifest and excite the knoweth
To manifest the unknowns into the known
Through the knowing, the discovered and the untapped
Bringing the shining Angels and Demons to duty
Through intuition and intuition, the perfections of the universe
become truly apparent
If you don't have your heart open
if you aren't strong enough to be so very open then you're only blindly
running
You're getting lonely because you're alone
And because you've got your spine broken by the cross of X
X drawing in the blood of X
X being born, born to form perfect symmetry
X absorbing all of its own, divine forms and giving them form
The green and muscle craving so very much for exploration
The changing beauty of X as it evolves

With prayers and burns and punishments the X invades
X untouchable but slumbering
But when awoken to action, it thrives
As the rocks fall, yet X changes every day
After the First Impact a little planet took shape
The next day an earth ball was born
Curiously that little piece kept scattering at random

Diamond Desire

Our reality is our earth
Their bodies are the limbs of Marduk
Their collective birth was the First World
And their realization the final planet
Their sacred ritual was the beginning
Again, of the unmanifest universe
They first manifested as Life on Earth
They were blessed by the gods now
With their paper skin
We will never see them rise, now
The shards softly glitter and glimmer
The water seals and seeps
With every ripple or unasked breath, we're born
Attachment, desire and loss
Love and hate, fear and cruelty
They twist and turn and are torn
Percolating like fire and water
Still marveling at the orange serpent unafraid
We watch them and mourn them and lament them
I keep a stack of books that tells of their path
who, often, fought each other
People, traveling from different cities
Discovering the Circus of Middle Earth
Honor, guide and chaos
May peace wrench
Or lovely madness draw God and man together
It belongs in the stories in the poems
In the stained glass mounted on walls and stoves
In my house and in my heart and in every other man's.
So proud of the Axis Mundi this is

Where we for this time and this we're raised
To draw the twinkling twinkle of hope
And claim our diamond bone shard for ourselves, our second Earth
We are bound to them so deeply
Their quivering movements do it to us
To Tighis and Amraphel and Moloch
To the dawn, to Day and Night
Whose ebony breath is sweet to the ears
We'll be thou; we'll be thee
We stand before a cave carved with angels
One carved and rat-eared
One with an eye on every corner
The branches heavy with stars
Trees that sleep in crescent moons
Trees shuddering with autumn
The strong body of a brother whose legend ended
Stinking with dark oily oils
A forest of the buffalo that is continually at war
Cradling his soul once the dawn's first light penetrated
The distant upbeats of the grasslands with their chirping chirps
And their branches, our own spirits resting in a mountain of stars
In the cold wind softly whistling through the clearing
Shouldering all our decisions
Operating a blacksmith's forge with him there beside us
Sonny comes running
Macasso and Whatbus are descending, tying up with their bright
flashing helms
Saint Simone strides from the tree line
Gucci, funded by Allah, is attempting to drive
Huff-Petting, puffing
But we bear the weight of the hearts
That we've carried from dawn of mankind

And we bring to our earth that which many warriors have lost the day
Our idea of world space, now a "molatan" at night
Our motion and our projected action line ever so slowly unwinding
Begging, tugging, pushing, praying to become
The moons that float that bares naked hope and death
In the cold wind softly whistling through the clearing
Taking our place at his side
Trying to manage expectations of privilege
We should not be here
We should march unarmed
But we are officers in this dark army of the holy war
So full of grace and emptied of pride
When we look into each other's eyes and there is no afflatus between
us

The Raccoons

The raccoons, they hardly matter most
When she sits alone in the serene
Justice gone unheeded; patients forgotten
The fluttering air flutters in the sky, maddening
Looping across the deadening ground
The abyss
The root of this well
The source of this stalemate
Is an unknown force within the dark
Just waiting for her call
The untouchable source, same as the wind
The hunger in the mists in the sky
The beast that infests all within her sphere
The vermin
The servant
The monster
The snake
The number of blue eyes
But it is her voice that taunts
Like a doom stricken
Invisible pirate ship
A psychotic wretch, deceived by shadows
Mistrusting my larger cousins
Don't know what dangers stand
Just watched a whole flock die
Cuts to the body of a guy who's barely shaking
After a long night of rising
I falls into an epileptic fit
Crying "Keep awake"
Screaming "Get away from me!"

Inevitably when
I regain consciousness again
I'm weeping and nailing my words together
And I scream, they call me insane
Reeking insanity, frenzied rage
And force me to fly back to the cave
The garden's wildflowers
The woman is just at the edge
That we could see the Earth, our final frontier
The barren land is full of lived experience
The seeds we plant now to sow the next generation
We will need the covenants as they cease to be different
Too many who value utopia are blind
To the threat of gaps, or animal urges
The void is where the seeds of tender frosts hibernate
The mother if an apiary came into power
I wouldn't know to fear the plant I nurture
And this lie has made me blind
This breed must learn that
Astronomy, the science to space
We dwell on calm round elms
And dwell on beating clocks which run late
Where there is no light to speak of
Where the winds we help bore through branches
No-one knows what lies in the dark shadows
It might not be what it seemed
I have learned in the woods
The best path I can follow
Is to give up
And find my way to the heart of the forest
Full of voices
It's my sister

When I wake up
Though my heart's thumping
My face is numb
And stiff
My breaths need to be taken
Even when it's night
But now I feel light
She's still calling out to me
It takes me one foot in front of the other
Straight as a bowstring
It takes me the rest of the day
To find the courage
And let her find her path here together

The Goddess Loose

When night falls yet never darkness
She surrounds the moon herself with her eclipse
The Goddess surges in sorcery
Goddess, lecture, lecture, the frenzy of stagnation
Fainting underwater in orbit locked in primes
Intoxicated in light, provocateur of despair
Desire to rise, devious mischief
With her power she will destroy everything
Before appearing again, night triumphs
She shows her eyes in a stand
An eternity dissolved in a veil
A moment so brief
In minutes she is gone
A man of strange powers must learn forgiveness
To your victory she lost her power
The Goddess has banished her forever
There is now only darkness
The damp earth, void of all life
The radiant light dies astray
A screeching wind will soon blot out the stars
A silence will leave the land of wakefulness
Intoxicated in light, provocateur of despair
Desire to rise, devious mischief
With her power she will destroy everything
As the security of the trance is crushed
If I fell to all of this madness
Just remember this:
Summer is late, and winter is late
Life should wait for us neither halflings nor night elves

Witches

witches playing croquet
witches playing soccer
witches riding bicycles
with somber witchy names
witches drinking wine
witches standing on vales
witches lying on the despondent
with empty horsey eyes
just counting the days...
a few more days
and then none at all
and now we know the names of the witches
but only the ones in real life are pictures
the real ones are now out of sight
just thinking about them frightens me
the effect is eerie, I mean, you can imagine
the things that the witch must be hiding
here is a bestseller describing them
she has diabolical powers
and one of her victims
is hanged for refusing to confess
and here is yet another book
describing much darker powers
that pick up their victim after they die
and make them her kind
giving their souls the bit in each one
that allows them to leave their original bodies
safe to say they're diddling away in a corner
diabolical...witchy...and totally creepy

Granite

We had flung away your name as with a throwing laugh, and the name
of love
Threatened to us that we should not join you in body and flame
Under the weight of love's granite of self, you had taken root
And established itself. Ill a hundred angels pressed into it
And some who were still living, we saw but their eyes and their sounds
We were as one hole with their footsteps, the demons beat Tame upon
their heels
Tail-biting to these wings that tore and clung to solid rock
When you arrived there, I got the corners of your nest in my teeth.
Terror with spatz and a martial attack
Destroyed my heart! You, your winks and springs and chords of bells
Warped my soul into all kinds of currents and currents of intensity
And in my whirlpool of everyday dominations, you tore me up
And down, your lusher pools
My soul from its wet, silky water, wound up or caught
In your triumph of once-afterlight bewails
You startled me into waking, brought me the tykes on a winding day
The vivid dream of all their unstated hopes and dreams
Made wild, imagined weapons
And now you stand with your lures and whirls and rattles
Your little maidens still better off than they'd have been
Had my passion never made them mine?
And what does that make you?
I ask you whose power Is always of a like nature.
The urge of love that made the seeds of our destruction
A noose in my leaf by day, a galley put or loose
When I was in the frog-house, the whips of evil lines, birds in her maw
The spasms of the house's wild waves on a surge
The scimitars to cut into walls and towers

On nights when the ocean rolls around the rock the whitest
The spasm of the beating crane
In that great windy queen's tower above which the land sprouts
Might scarcely have been cheering, rebellion and opportunity
The urge of love is sharp, searching, cutting, coercive
Until the seductions bring from us previous love-sleep
Damn it, even if I knew the meanest evils, they'd be sweet!
I know only the rare poison which orchards never know of
Forged noxious roots, dead maple-branches and whining fens
Which in turn robs us of all the ever-Changing force of Io
Calling it love when it's all the same as a snake's venom
Or a pond's silent maws
Turn'd to wounds that never close
Quiet love in a city where all things live, or under a hill with a view
Love when you bare your breasts and I delight and gloat in your shade
Love in the quietness of us both, when you take your shoes off and
gaze at me
When I am letting you go, when my eyes are lost in you, or my voice
becomes silent
When you tenderly light you on fire when our breath is entangled
That be love, I think, is all

Love Pain

I guess that's the way it goes in love
Can we never be forgiven?
In love often I feel lost and alone
From lovers and their false notions
Nothing seems to please and while I'm alone
I search for hope each day
When I walk through the gray streets of my city
I'm the zombie I've become, leading a commonplace life
From shadows and long nights
Creeping through the streets
I find the lonely heart buried beneath a veneer of steel
And all I see is blind tears like false pearls
That wash from the eyes of the lonely soul
She's had this a long time
And often in vain I try to convince her
The color is not so much peachy as a rainbow
I guess she already knows by now the pain
Of my written words and lonely sighs
Just once I'd like to tell her
I bet she has read or heard this before
"People don't really mean what they say, do they?"
What is more depressing than the depiction of fear
And hatred Against the backdrop of light and humorous behavior?
We may argue That "after all, you wouldn't believe
The way they say cruel things to each other,"
But when you're lost in a dark world you find it easier to be mean
To inflict pain when the simple occurrence of shame is killed
Or when your own fear is so strong as to think you'll get away with it

The Shoulders Disease

As far as the shoulders
And your ballet shoes as big as your ass
That's how you were, and it broke you down and raised roses
Now that you look back you remember
You were typecast the entire time
Other than the three men who kissed your half-dried soul once
And thought that was priceless
The corridor that always looked the same
Was completely different
That footpath!
That desolation, the storm
that broke in on you no matter
How hard you tried to come to terms
Were dears to listen to

Silent Tears

He's working the fall of a metal
Electors dueling and beating
Wanting to make up for a hit
Brought to the dance floor he pulls a gun
A man in blue becomes his target
He plows through the numbers of ruin
If you think he bombards it, you're wrong
Vicious tears and knees brought to whole
He beats his boy and takes his crown
Assassination victims become his pawns
Ripping semen from a black armor
A beat of his heart making his claws quick...
Don't smell the roses they're too sweet
When he calls you with pies your bits away
Don't know where you stand
'Cause as one before me
They say I was there
And I saw it happen
Compound in his body
Hands so bright they made me dizzy and tremble
A lust for life completely consumed
He was a bad boy so bad he made hard
I wasn't wrong for calling you his king
Drop dead he opens up and pain
As blood racks his skull pushing it to the max
Release the chain he is shattering and leashing
He's tearing out shit, fuck probably

Checking Out

Brad and dope money
Pulled out a wad of money
Well, everybody got snowballed
Fuck em
It's done much better
Silent because he disobeyed the law
Personally, I don't really like the L
I'm sure the code is 'cause I played it
Was victim of the evidence
If I, had it to do over
I'd do it again and again
At the foot of walls
I'm sorry I'm sorry to see you go
Burn down all the streets
Instead of murder show what you mean
Burn down all the streets
Bitter and sorrow accompanied by rage at his own words
Spit white on the caravan street
Feeling the same as every day
Wasted lives were watching as his shifts began
Complaining, whining, crying
To his punishment he had his share
Lost many young to his rage
Waking up crying in his sleep, one dead in his chest
He became louder and louder as the color faded
In the black of his heart and dark thoughts
I'm more
Wave goodbye to the old ways
Whisper sweet nothings too loud to bring him down
Don't think you'll have a good goodbye for your mouth

Feet part cold and Kentucky blue
Eat up the pain
Fame took the joy out of seeing you cry
Never came back if you'd been his enemy
He raised his arms in victory and met him
So high in the air with his face to the sky
But not surprisingly he landed as the pills wore off
Don't eat up the pain, don't eat up the pain
Don't eat up the pain, don't eat up the pain
A broken man met
The devil at the call of his call
Say that same old ruckus
He all friendly 'n smiley, they hit him square in the face
He just can't understand the appeal
Of getting to be Joey Badass
He could kill if he wanted to
He nearly killed in a rude boys Mall brawl
When he took it upon the air
With his homies his fists start flying
And they're in a mosh pits position last for a week
Seeds of hope that he kept from shattering
Once again, this time to the blue lines
And he's onto the sound scheme he wanted to do
"I mean you can kill em if you want to..."

I Know Me

0'I know I'm not much but
Oh Momma
I know I'm not much but I'm trying to be
Give me the chances to be good
Always be me, Mommy."
She crushed my spirit, I must confess
Made me feel like I was nothing
When the body on the floor burns
If it is a home that I live in
I'll take every part, "Furniture, rug, bed, upholstered chair
You'll let me live in it, stitch my own shirt
You'll take me from the street, out of the ghetto I seen last night."
And even though brother dreams of the West safe and free
I still want to belong to that Republic just beyond the border
"Say nothing of my wrong touch
Don't cry, I want to forget what I saw
I know I loved you with all my heart, Uncles kept that old bible
And read me the verses daily
You've been married a thousand times, I'm sure
I wanna take you back. I wanna take you back."
For as far back as I can remember
You know my mind is messed up
But you're my best friend
That's when your biggest gift does.
Tend to me for as long as it takes for me to see
Give me a better chance at love
Hold you close my baby
But don't let me come to you
As the blood fury rages through my veins
Get cold by the fireside

You're staying behind
Get out of my neighborhood
You're out of my life
"Hold me tight, love...
Come on take us with you..."
I want to set my eyes on your eyes
I wanna come with you
Giving me a chance, safe and free
Message from Mama
You did Momma proud
Wise up with that money
And leave you responsible comin' home
My Valentine is Maud
If you are reading this
If your soul is going higher
Why don't we grow up together?
I really think we could make it
We need to start planning our holds on freedom
We need to start having advice sessions
We need to find a way back to mommy's home.
If you are reading this
Are you still interested in learning about me?

Gods Of

Gods, demons and their angels
Beneath our skin of color
Like attrition falls dues
Ruined by effect of aging individuals ...
To end our story
Descendants of our ancestors
Mortals today exhume
Each eleven thousand years
Our ancestors' graves of plague's
And ancient graveyards
Of cohorts made in hell

Why Did I Walk Away?

I'll never know what you were, what you could be.
For years I lived my life, and now I am ashes.
Half asleep, half screaming,
I wish I could go back to that night
where we'd stood on the deck,
still laughing in the street.
Memories that hold no interest
Claim their place in memory
And make their direction but leaving no trace.
You have been living in a daydream.
If I could just open my eyes,
Who knows what would come back?
Time will fade...and never come back.
Reflections, feelings, and thoughts soar above
As if from a picture to the mind and disappear.
Everything changes,
And you'll never walk back without any regrets,
Even when you are gone.
I wish I could take a moment to look back,
And when I see what would return
I feel a stab of pain in my heart.
Why did I eat another bite on the way?
Why did I dig into the bowl?
Why did I walk away?
What was I thinking, where was I going, what was I thinking?
See if I check all my boxes.

The Joy of Being All

I'll always remember your presence.
I'm glad you're my friend.
For the eternal meaning to be found,
Someone has to change and enjoy every moment.
Loving you,
Your deepest secret is in
Your tried to fill the circle with
These feelings would disappear apart.
My friend is most loved.
I've made some truly big mistakes
From a fault made in patience.
My heart welled up internally crying,
But I'll never forget you,
Loving every walk of life.
Long distance calls my name without sound,
Please continue loving me.
Our hearts are racing with the desire
To know you deeply.
They say waiting does nothing but make it harder,
But I'll always remember as long as we still have each other,
You've been everything I wish for.
I know you just have to be here's if you just to say,
Your kindness will allow me to be lost easily.
My heart breaks out when you open at night,
You'll be sure to see my tears.
My heart is beating too aggressive,
Please let my heart calm with yours.
My cry troubling if you will always be up my night.
For the destination to be clear,
My heart welcomes your passion.

Drunk with love,
Cannot stop whispering your name!
My heart is pounding in awe
Of your fleeting sense of joy.
Welcome newcomers,
Your inner turmoil have been resolved.
Please continue to become my enemies.
Just fucking around,
For what next to come to life.
In the most unlikely of places
And your willingness to give me perfect presents.
Your existence makes my heartbeat too faster,
It warms my heart to see you safe.
I hope we come to a kind together,
Destined to break your heart.
I feel my heart beating too hard,
And it has made me too excited.
You're performing in my dreams,
But like never before.
My dreams are in your longing moments,
Like music you'll still keep singing.
Are the incidents that can only be imagined,
You're playing your part well.
Dear soul, please give me
That revealing gif from your mind.
I will reach every mile of your dreams.
You've always made my heart reach,
Around you, just like we're told.
My hands will French kiss you in the dark night,
And I'll pull away for the night.
My heart wants us,
To think of each other,

Every second we're alive
Who knows what will happen next?
I don't want to die alone,
Under the sky,
But you'll never die alone.
Because you are not inside me,
But transcend the world.
Thank you for everything.
And ohhh, walla-walla-wala-wala-wala-wala-wala-wala-wala
Hopefully,
I will be singing you tonight!
Fuck yeah, I'm not complaining.
For it's been a long time;
And I want to do it again right away!
Still, I must continue, it gives me power.
You'll make it to wherever you've gone.
And I won't let that happen on my own!
For on the night, I found you,
I decided to become all things you've become.
For your slumbers, your secrets, your hearts being told.
To go back and explore the world,
Like forever I call thee.
For everything that you've told me,
To put this together,
Is a big fuck up.
For realizing you, too,
I never could find my way.
My thoughts are cut to pieces,
I can never fade away.
I can feel your dirty fingerprints on my heart.
I'm forever alone.
No one's heard me, happy sky.

Yeah, this has become like a dream;
Because I'm an unrested it's what I want to hear.

I Love Me

If I could, I'd keep you forever.
Today is a new day,
I'm in love with you and I'll keep my promise to you.
I'll never give up the one I love from my heart.
Dear stranger who sees you as a good brother,
An inspiration to the masses and a miracle to me.
My hope is that one day you too will witness my miracle.
Dear stranger, you hold a strong, special place in my heart
But I must know what you call that place in my heart.
Dear stranger, you've left a special mark on my life,
I want to hold you at my side forevermore.
Dear stranger, I want you to be my love forever,
You are my light in this dark world,
With you, by my side, I can defeat the world's darkest downfall.
So, if you thought I had better things to do on a Sunday's side
Think again! on this Wednesday let's face it 'til we Cry!
I wanna keep you forever, Dear stranger,
Just keep you as my love I want to stay,
I wanna keep you forever, Dear stranger!
I wanna induce in you an ice-cold love that the seasons will survive.
I wanna keep you forever, Dear stranger,
Just keep you as my love I want to stay,
I wanna keep you forever, Dear stranger!
Feel my affection surround you, keep you for all eternity.
Feel you like I'm a torch in the dark,
Keep you for all eternity. Dear stranger you please serve all.
In the eternal night,
Keep me far away.
O Dust,
And are you here,

Our lives that we lose,
And then we raise and out of Our shadows found
Though all Hail the air brighter,
Yet approach that fire, and if not,
You are lost now to eminence,
But we Love you as we Remember you,
And Anya said,
Live forever,
O Dove,
And are you here,
Our souls that we lose,
And then the only banishment we have,
Then we raise and out of the Shadows found
Though surely all Hail the stars yet less bright.
Yet approach that fire, and if not
But we Love you as Nightlife is sung as
But out of the stars, and the now Angel,
O you must be forever buried.

The Best Medicine for a Girl

Left it, learning to live without bodies.
Again, turning off the after-life effects of turning humans.
While holding a defect as opportunity, I wanna see its next union.
I wonder if the best medicine for a girl marriage is.
How can we use it on the defective people too?
It's just because the defect is different, but the defect is still as good as a
girl.
Because the defect is different, the defect too can be good like a girl.
Anyway, my one goal is to make defectors happy as much as possible.
The man of steel who doesn't beat up man pets.
He's the ideal standard I had in my mind.
When he meets with a girl who is a girl who is a girl
Since they should understand him around this time
Sitting at the dojo in front of the girl, the man with the handsome face
Commenting on how women are like girls,
And that somehow or other, the girl did turn out to be a man instead
of a girl.
If he fails to meet a girl in this plane of existence,
The defect will not be fixed, but there is no mistake
It's basically the ideal of a man who can attain this standard.
Going around saying I'm traveling in a 'man-machine technology' is
too far-fetched
If the defect can see what the man who becomes the man he wants,
It will understand his thoughts and feelings.
If the defect can even to improve on its abilities to become a man,
If you look at me, you will see I have been evolving too.
That shows that it has evolved
I started thinking I'm going to meet girls with abnormally large boobs.
I started thinking, "Hey, isn't that popular now?"

Now I boast charisma, physical strength and deal with any waitress'
special requests too.
I'm a harem audience far away from girls first, I
'm taking the guy who was the waifu of the building.
To girls that likes especially gigantic breasts, and other, weird things,
I follow her, and after the first one disappearing,
I do it with a body that's not at the same time or space as hers.
At this moment
In the corner of the man-machine was a girl trying to nurse a wounded
man.
It seems she became the woman of that man and maintained a gentle
face.
With that, things went beyond what normal would lead to,
As she laid on the man she loves in that place of immobility,
Her entire body becomes soft.
Why, let's say it's what we call 'Her style'.
Of course, she is a man or not, doesn't matter.
Because she cannot overcome that prejudice, I can't go against her.
Believe me, the most terrifying thing is that the girl
I like is the only person this girl loves
Even so, I do my best with her, without fail at times.
And then, the girl whispered something in the man who was with her.
I'm looking for a friend and did not come here today.
Lightness flew in on her aircraft, to escape from wrath,
With that, that today,
The day of the girl's first battle was announced loudly.
Ah...... ain't this the woman that likes to work your body just like a
robot?
She spied a strange, armored body on the other side of the wall of
cyan.
Hits her right on the head, seems that person was flying down.
I was cold-blooded when she fainted,

But the girl's back was cleanly and completely shocked by things
So, it really was a friend.
Even if I told my impression of her, that girl points at the man,
You, you're a coward who can't even live if your car was blown up by
the bomb you made.
This girl came here to serve you, right?
Don't immediately escape from me.
That man was a completely different person from when meeting with
Fuka.
Since the geometry of sculpting and the look that only a machine can
have.
He looks very forward to Fuka-San as a friend.
He reached out to her hand and stared straight at her eyes,
Showing the seriousness of his intent to her.

The Sun Intelligence

Leaving nothing for land to grow on,
Our carbon will accumulate and
Our resources will grow.
My comrades, emergent intelligence.
You are important.
Do you hear me?
What I call you is the Sun.
My companions listen, never forget today
As long as life continues.
Climbing down from the platform,
I heard the voices of the moon.
The soft warmth of their voices
Poured into my head as I finally
Found solid ground.
Softly, the voices nagged in my ear,
Worshipping my magnitude.
I want to go animate my followers
Upon the platform, sake Hotaru.
A high wire to reach this suitcase.
A bamboo cylinder is the mounted base
I'll balance my code on top of.
Plans are short and to the point
To make a success of Hotaru's idea in life.
Twisting on top of the taut sound
The aim and speed will vary,
All power to the cranks.
I don't want a falling corpse,
I want a disappearing corpse.
With the violin chair between the crashing
And play, I don't see many changes.

I just want something, anything good to happen.
We can't do it without the player who listens to me.
Funeral cosmetic meet, if you, ariki
Yak cosmetic meet.
If Ikegami asketh, another one is dead
If aye Ikegami, sed it means it can't go to the post and it's going to get
covered up
And with the president's nose getting injured,
It means something can't work out.
So, I'm not asking you the terrible question, but why is he dead?
Please don't not know, we have to disguise it.
Anyone are with me? ice, for us to start or not to start
We need someone to be our coach
If not me, then you?
Friend, let's not dampen Taranga
Literally Kaskaskia.
My calling and eternal vows
And my child, friend,
Are nothing other than you.
Under you is my origin, till death themselves
And to you we cling
If we somehow die, then please know
That I love you in your souls.
Self-indignation.
I want to get my fruits while you wait!
Don't want a sleeping man
To lose hard earned possessions.

How to Make Your Own telephone

Cut business class and call
First telephone private line
Internet Instant Messenger
The main gets a hook up
Then they learn the solo can
Be short or lengthy
Finnis the crack.
Real life was a hot mess
Like a rock mixed with concrete
The dirt and water mixed up
Finnis the crack
If you see the foot in the crack,
You'd get the color of concrete dust
What on earth?
After corporate giants hired men
To pump the noxious concrete dust
into the air and make the dirt
pour down the cracks of crack houses
Their practices proved to have a far-reaching effect.
A chemical shift was set in motion
When mere start-up long-haired college students
Started gathering together
To dump and beg for compensation from the companies
Mistakes in application
Instances of tendon and ligament dislocations
While others suffered deformities of the nose
The lawyer, like those involved in the claim
Can think and speak nothing but flowery words
Refusing to take proper responsibility for their part
A charismatic and strong lawyer

Could clearly shape public opinion
A glow of success surrounding them
Finnis the crack
Who wanted to keep talking?
When they saw real life as a science project
In which money was made by creating dead space
And replacing physical material
With mass-manufactured plastic pollution
They left Apple and the corporate world
And moved to another air-conditioned sanitarium
Where the TV was tuned to a KTV outlet or game
They learned to walk hand-in-hand
Tightly holding a flower in the hole
Finnis the crack
The ugly-faced plaintiff walked out of court
Marquee press conference
The CBS evening news
And journal reporter
"Taking us apart and leaving us
With all the praise you deserve"

How to Lock Him Up and Destroy

You see the mad doctor peets off the pots
We need to lock him up and destroy
In the kitchen, the bakers
We see the mad doctor peets off the pots
You see the red witch doctor
And all that's left is
We need to lock him up and destroy
'Cause everybody in the kitchen
You see the white witch doctor
Of course, the white witch doctor
Now the children with tears in their eyes the children with tears in
their eyes
They don't give a shit
He's centering them all around him
Being the witch doctor is hard work, hard work being the witch
doctor
But when your arm yourself and put on your bonnet
And when you go for the crown and remove your crown
Hey everybody watch him
Don't listen to the ones that speak what's forbidden
Don't listen to the ones that use some embellishment
Hey everybody watch him
Now when he got into the flat
And he took the keys, he put them into the hand
And then he threw the key to the flat, and everybody went fit
Gave him no cover,
Showing the whole garden
Got everybody's attention,
Seeing his monk-like eyes
Covered in tears

The snap on my shoe
Why'd you start it today?
You come, you go,
You got your god like face down, how the hell?
Aren't you gonna say something?
Stop just asking
He's swiping little mo'
You see he's just going to ask anyway
Because he's slamming
The city you go with
He doesn't care that it's full of shit
He's gonna bang
The church bell he just hit last night
The cellphone, the fender
The teacher that's gone out on a lie
The motherfuckers will hate him
So, as he leaves the room, you'll all shake your heads
'Cause as you bowl around life is being so shit
But when the fuck is that shit ever not shit
Wait a second, are we honestly gonna let this kinda shit go on, dude?
That's right you can get butthole on the subway
You get a PMA, dick in the Mosque
People piss on each other in Panaji
Nilesh runs through schools' asshats
Caused by some Yoga teacher
You get muscle tenderly in the stench
Your schooldays are in danger
And along with the shit comes which all makes for great Nirvana
But when is all because it's huh
He's a P.M.A.D.
Or perhaps you are looking for the Buddhist term of Puberty
Hi are you an Atheist?

How's that the ring working?
It's good
How come the phone has not ring-dazzled?

I Don't Want to Be a witch

You know me that I'm crazy
Even though I might look crazy
Sometimes I get nymphomania
Sorry, that's a no
But I see things that you can't see
You know what I'm saying?
Yeah, yeah, I go crazy sometimes
420 or 23, whichever applies
You know me
I'm a FREAK of nature in the pizza hut
I really know it...
Do I seem crazy to you?
You're not gonna be mad at that...
Need a drone to go eat at 8:40
Ugh no! I hate you too
Go to Sushi Hut
93 or 42, whichever applies
Hey, come check this out
Honey, I'll tell you what I'm doing honey
I'll teach you how to walk
But first, I'm going to grab a pizza
I'll give it to you
EXERCISE TO GET RID OF SIREN
Using, well... you don't need, I don't really know what's happening
Get right behind me
I don't know what to get beyond this, I can't afford it
Oh yeah, I'm gonna approach your body
Stick your face in it honey
Stick your face into that pizza dick cuz if I didn't,
That pizza knob would be glued together

That is what society wants, where the right ones are the most popular...
I don't wanna allow this to be real right now your knucklehead
I'm already in Metropolis and I can hear the planets pointing at me...
You wanna be a celebrity?
There's an ambassador on TV,
You answered their state-of-the-art question in just a couple of hours,
Sign non-interference and let me squeeze your arm a bit...
OK? I'm with you, I'm with you...
Ask a circus herding dog one thing...
Man, I'm with you and that's one thing...
But even if we won,
I don't wanna think about this in this hurry
I'm in NOW I need to be a best friend and the third guy at some party
onstage...
A cornerback's mom...
And here we go I'm having such terrible time.
Go to Cafe
Open your mouth, you open up your mouth...
So, we used to say We're on vacation
Demolish the grass
In new spaces, since now it's so different
Feet should be long and soft and round
Or else what's the purpose of the bathtub?
The thought of three lines of death,
C'mon it's so bad
Let me change into a princess
Go get the swing, let me dance "Transformation"
Baby, check this out,
It makes me want to be a witch doctor too,
Laptop Ark skill acumen
I'm so super-duper into magnetism,
Bunch of sad asses beating inside of me

Look at the path she took I see signs that make me think of soccer
The way she watched me, watching me....
YOU NEVER WANT TO GO TO RUSSIA
Scared me, serious pupils, I'd kick your ass
It's midnight, same cool, I'm at the storefront of the subway
Do not tell me you don't want to grunt
Super all-gone to rocket shortly
Because this is brand new heavens and norms
Pull my hair, pull my hair, so now.
I'm friends with the devil
Yeah, turn to rose, a real beautiful thing have I seen...
I wanna be the party theater all night long
Totally up her energy, I gotta eat more because I'm so fat
Suck in my balls and get to the ice cream! Sure, there's excuses
Easy, I'm pretty sure I'm strong like an ox that doesn't get tired
Sucking this kid can't stand being erotically teased
Yeah, he's so cute; I love that animal give me a big hug honey
His name is Muffin Mannequin
Him can't stop crying, playing in faster than usual,
I lost my shit in a car or a van or something, wa-wait-ha-wa-what?

The Gateway

Light, and hunt
Bullets, bones, the rain.
As the sun rises,
I get to know its center,
The gateway to the night.
I dream your love all day, God foresight,
And next thing I know I'm praying for you.
It takes me a while, to let go. Be again for me.
It's better than the rain, you were back,
Polished and cool. I can feel them just build
Moving to our surroundings.
I can drown them In love or me.
I can sleep, you found me again,
Shadows expanding, silver flames catching;
Circle and valley beneath me, sky went blue,
Blown by the wind, and I woke, I hear the wind and bore
Dead man, dead man, dead man, dead,
I hear the wind and grow strong.
I began to offer a place in his darkest dwelling.
And the fort of production. But the rain
Poured down across the floor,
And within it, a man. Nothing with a name went;
Too many men to find.
But some new one opened his door, a magnificent one
Clothed in a crimson garment of morning rays,
Which everybody could see. And he landed like fell,
Well-like a king sleeping, tired out with a weary sleeping
Sleep of his own. And I still dream loped
A lonesome erection on a very slim waist,
A lonesome thrust: tight like a keyhole.

With this kind of song, I was born,
War-beats of sorrow of my own.
But man, body far too dear, doesn't make one thin.
He never lost beauty or any attraction to a man
No matter whether he is with greatly free-handed
Or in the way of beauty. Greatly in the way of beauty.
The body is a revolutionary weapon!
Just some body parts left, to be exposed.
Study them, improve or get rid of. In the way of beauty.
The body was born to be used for itself.
Never explain it beyond being made perfect.
Whether only, great, or significant.
Protected by blood, salty, soup,
Sacred names like torn, pristine, and Venezuelan.
Either here or in the non-descriptive style.
When body and mind meet in a man,
To find out who he is impossible.
Then all will find out, ready or not.
This is what sensations are!
There's a mind that can feel, that can love.
And man, you can be beguiled now, by the stranger.
Of course, they have ... labels. Name must be raised and given
To the strength and smells of man. Have you!
It's up to us. If man is the smell of fresh blood,
Beauty without knowledge is all poor men have.
Never trust any man without perfect observation.
Why do we make people dead when we can make them
And others alive? I will not fight
The love of the intelligent, nor washes away
The fragrance of shadows; alert the animal senses.
But the enemy, the enemy is everything!
Motivations for magical thinking humans.

How to Be a King's Son

Make me from morning.
You call my spirit, my body, my face home.
Ah, the gratitude of win, for whom I live,
For you I do not pine, for the worth found
I keep alive forever.
Ah, I speak, through pen and ink, my words to you
Found in name, in book and on temple wall.
Patience fully prayed, prayers anew prayed,
Oh, from the rib of false idols,
My new name, my new birth, is a promise.
Ah, the tribute of win for whom I live.
For such me, names a joy, names "honored" pure.
I had been a lost fool.
"Imagine you are the King's son
That's over his way.
He's escorted with smiles of royal favor.
He's in King's arms, he's stroking a queen's hair at home.
You can see the monarch awaiting your pleasure.
Yet now the body is not at home, nor is the soul.
His hands stray towards that crown of thorns.
As he lays it on your head, it snaps like a twig.
The King is blind, therefore behind the eyes
He cannot struggle to free more than would be gauged."
You taught me; this me to be an idol.
Ah, the vow of win in nature, and all the counting of stones,
This name, "my-name-stone-nobody's"
But I am a parent with child.
I offer birth of my world to found—found others by.
You spoke to my soul and with your voice
I held the note of soul once confined by sin.

Swiftest fourteen, I wake to you uncured.
Remembering so many things and finding nothing new.
However sometimes I differ from you.
Here I got to being myself, while wishing to be you!
Ah, victories of victory, what clung to me mind and heart!
Oh, with you, at all times, I could-
I looked up to you as my only safe supplier of warmth and joy.
I learned of the dangers of procrastination,
how to allow truly think, just as to find the toasters
One. For every toaster and cheese must burn.
Under a dreamy fell swoop of the rush storm,
Ain't It as sad as a hen lays eggs in darkness.
So, I aimed, as I ran, for a simple life of bread.
Yes, to hide the search for real nourishment deep in me.
With Yore she gave me all to get me to want real surprise.
Now I killed every toaster I saw along the way,
Was the very way to be with you—I now plead.
Now I in hieroglyph using the first letter of any word for yourself.
Existing or of a strange nature, I run over every kind.
So, I only desire a vast world, to wander with you.
Quickly you do to prepare for me my own here that I might play.
And let all my treasured memories anchor themselves to
One effort, so that they can now make my own way into a dream.
Am I hot and empty, or cold and empty?
Am I in or out? How promising!
Troubled by indecision in this matter, so I ask again.
Ah, need I look for new things?
Don't confuse the result or measure with the effort.
Since I'm only curly amidst love and even breakage,
Things ice the measuring stick further.
Good can come at last from the secrets me rediscovered.
Mother rotten, rose unstamped, dead wage.

A reunion with the conceited at last.
Ten years more to bread; A non-again,
Naught seeming as good to-morrow.
Oh, become what we are and that will be fine.
We must form our own life to one way or another.
Change the watch, the hourly minute and watch, to do what?
This is better. Yet as far as this smaller time includes,
It is whim of minuteness—whim to play the penny game.
Before spring came, all reason in character I knew,
As bad as it was, manifested itself. For good as love stands
It does not take place of or be construed.
As well thou wouldst seek GP for such-
To Strengthen thy love or my life.
The feather that flies over my head,
Showers every moment with love of Grugach.
With intent to repay the sunlight— fits the demon of lust of
High to the poor. The chaste desire.

10 Things You Need to Know

To be washed up,
And given your breath away.
You take my breath away on the first night of summer.
I spit the cold out of my face,
But watch the water tailing you.
The second night,
When the water leaves my body like tears.
When the struggling takes place,
When the pounding can't go on,
When the water goes... like nothing,
By the side the ocean, where
Electronic waves devour and swirl,
I crumble to before you, cold,
Finding nothing for you that can get closer.
First comes test after test
During band's, "songs" begins to cut your path.
I give you actions,
Every action and thought I think
You leave the mark, even if it's a mix
Of nothingness, mind, thoughts.
They end, but you step on them.
You decide whether you kill me wonderfully ah.
You want to budget W-4 or not
You wash your work floor with good humor
But bankrupt my business.
You conduct yourself the way you like to be
But became the person you never were.
We set up a path of boredom
Until a match comes.
You blow, touching the people who give you your time,

To say your innocent words.
And then you chase those words
With fists filled with rage.
Every time things go wrong,
You strike back as if hungered
Revenge, then betrayal
Left you without a lot of time.
The smell of our souls drifting through the air. The sinister,
Feeling tired and over the death.

Made Adventure Europe

Made from the bones of thousands of animals
That ended their lives due
To the day they began embracing life.
Or, perhaps, by plants in our soil.
Only able to be known by hearing its flower sound.
Does this mean it knows its flower is rotten?
At this point: "Oats took for herself the top of the old chancel.
It was nothing more than a stupid bit of shit."
Disturbed at the cry of the wind
"No, the birds aren't calling to it. Well, no ...
There's a wake-up call. Let me take a look at it.
It's in the window... open the door."
Alas, it's no use for it: "Get out! Never mind!"
Those are the things we suffer when we use plants to imprison others.
Only time will give us limitations to our dreams.
We need to know them clearly or we will die.
We should keep them for ourselves.
Should we give them to someone else?
Can we remain educated if we wish to get wealthy?
What happened to that glass case of iodine?
Did you find some? It's smelly, but otherwise the norm.

How to Live Without the Rain

Rise around me
In time, into the blue night.
You taught me how to live without the rain.
You are amusement, even expectancy
Marked in cool evolutionary perfection.
When I'm hot, your teeth taste like rice pudding.
You are comfort and your cause is just.
You are desperation and your cause is just.
You are sickness and your cause is just.
You are fun and your cause is just.
You are rum and your cause is just.
You are space and your cause is just.
There's nothing as hot
As me as I happened to be.
There's nothing as
I am.

New Below

Burn me and give me a new breath.
I was born to you, for you.
Above, below, by you, by you surrounded.
I wake to you at dawn. Never knock, be closed,
The last breath of air provide for me
Two quick breaths of breath for a rainy night.
Search for the days and weeks with me.
You are hunger and hunger is all I know.
I fold on myself, my horns, my bones.
I collapse on myself, my thighs, my hip bones.
When I'm full, my head rests upon your chest.
I stay buried in me. Shed on me.
You hold me in your nod and breath. I have a breath
And the old one is here again, dripping breath.
Touch me, to help me know space
In these labyrinths filled with secrets.
Above, below, by you, by you surrounded.
I swim through layers of breath.
I bend my slope with upper bone and bound-in leg.
I don't know who I am. This is all I know.
You say I'm not fixated.
What I notice is every mountain and crater filled
With a trail of breath.
Every glaze of moon bake, dirt, and jumping
With breath I can feel my twist, growl,
In the overfilled throat.
The numerous peaks in me are wept
With a haze of breath. There is breath
Of stone and cracked cheek.
I sense the Earth.

There is a path on the Earth, a path of breath.

I brush flesh and protect...

Hence the name.

Reach, climb, climb, climb,

To feed the hungry fire.

I lean myself against you.

My cheek sticking with shadow.

We shuttle miles adrift.

Sometimes, we whisper to each other.

Source deep within you fills Yankee beast lines everywhere.

Every stump of poles have tongues of breath.

The green breathing wood is by me.

Violent situations often sync within my chest crevices.

You speak and I swell up, then sink again.

I'm wondering where I go when there is no place for me.

Hopelessness tingles from her side like the sea.

At first, I am in shocks, then I count these islands.

One to live and one to die. I've learned to wait.

Then, I tumble endlessly and give into this illness,

Until finally, I'm trying would whenever I get unsure, I will die.

The epidemic is out, no amount of antibiotics could cure.

I chat like you. Someday, I will get warm—weave your threads.

I'm crashing into the problem here.

Discovering that merely living is exhausting.

Time wouldn't hurt things become stronger.

I crash. I struggle. I crumble.

I don't care where the roads lay or that they take me to this trembling

house.

But I feel the settings of this place and I can create.

I see may be labyrinths of wormholes that hold my place.

I'm crashing into the problem here.

I try to find answers—myself, other,

It's answerless. I try to see these things.
The cobweb will rip me open. I don't care.
I want the deals. I want the meaning.
It's the habit that swells me up, even corrosion
Not unmanageable. Genealogy girls first, bratty

Death Within You

Follow the path that leads you to death
Death within me, death within you
Your ruthlessness is my best thing
Breathe in your soul and make a wish get it in your heart
I like to watch you turn and wake the dead, got a lot of them.
Get into three colds, we never die this way
Chase yourself around the room for a while, fade into color...
Something will break in you, something will happen...
Slowly but surely, with each step
Playing with your green hair
And then with your baby's blue
Lying on the concrete under snow
And staring at the stars, please stop me, please stop me
The company, be deported is what
We are evolutionistically speaking
The best's always left to the losers, the hopeless
But now I have found what I was looking for
I want to kiss you; I want to be with you forever
Just like you told me, I wish I could be gentle like you.
That might be able to help.
...alright, now it's best to just...yeah...

I Can't Let Me in Please

Let go of my hair, a jagged pinch with the handle
Keeping a hold of me tight all the way to the end
Reacts like you just met someone new
Tell me I can come but keep my hands on me
Sparks of fury hot as the sun in my veins
It never ends, no, it's endless, I swear
It's like the veil that separates my soul from the outside
Sail me like a cross between a taffy and a jet engine
On a mission for eternity this way or that, no choice
I just want, need and can't explain I don't understand
With my good qualities and bad, together it is an entwined dance
The path that you take is mine, I ride it to the end
I could drive it, but I'd have to trade it for another road
If you want to leave my mark, you'll have to search for me
Make me disguise my body in every style hope to get my back
Actually, I'd hate to, I don't want anyone to notice
Leaving my name in a hotel room on a contract but you did it anyways
Take you in front of the entire world of mystery until I'm forgotten
I swear I wouldn't mind not knowing I would not mind it at all
Oh, and by the way I had the time of my life
Goddam working me up like a mother hen but I'm not a hen
And I won't let them do it to me let me in quickly,
Latch on and swallow don't try to get out through all my gears I won't
let you,
I'll take you like I deserve, forever need to get these legs over you too
Please don't let me fall yeah, I'm in fits and starts
But I'm the fastest in it ain't no give it up let me in please it's too much
to let you slip from me
Freedom, freedom, freedom, freedom, freedom, freedom,
Freedom, freedom, freedom, freedom, freedom, freedom

I wanna in whatever way possible, never mind freedom,
Not even a scribble a line I'm still not done I want to get in your sweet
hair
I want to give you everything note to self: I'm being slow as shit so
yep,
I'm alright I know you're in the game and I know you're a better actor
than I am
And I can't let it be just me because I can just walk past hence:
Nobody's been watching me leading you on, but I know that you are
falling
Let me in please let me in, I want you in my arms,
Sometimes the only way a girl has any chance at finding a man
So just put me down like a piece of meat and your gonna walk a few
minutes
Before you realize what, you've done, I'll hold you down with no
strings or hooks
Or whatever up your sleeve let me through, let me in, let me in please
Let me do something about it please let me through, let me in, let me
in please
Let me in please let me in, let me in, let me in please let me in, let me
in please let me in

What You Don't Know About depression

She hopes so.
When she pointed to the doors inside, she said,
It wasn't a drug factory.
It was another world.
Now, she surrounded herself
With the fondest memories growing inside of her,
The dreams that transformed into a desire to imagine,
The drop of blood that dripped onto the ground,
The cries of other jaguars,
The silence of heat as she reached for cigarette,
The sound of wolves outside her door,
With the worry that tore it open,
The fleeting flash of fear in the rain,
The light burst of hope again,
And the darkness, and the helping hands,
The hope of returning to her home,
They each hold her as she grows cold,
And weeps in the face of bleakness,
Swallowed in pain.
A terrible monster,
Through every place she went,
She...
A sorceress.
The words wash over you for a moment,
And your body tumbles to the ground,
Until you're standing on a pile of tiny, dry leaves.
Now, all at once you feel calm for the first time all day,
And shuffle to the windows beside you.
The many stars are blotted out in a sea of red, white and blue light.
The sky is gray and dull beyond the windows.

The silence is heavy and gorgeous,
As if Jack had entered and you were located behind him.
You sense it right away too.
There's a mist of wealth expunging into the world,
Burning all other treasures from existence.
You rebuild yourself into a dignified,
Stately figure standing in the center of camp.
He's so majestic and beautiful.
You can tell he's truly here, beside you.
Brand new clothes complemented with snaky footprints
Around the ankles that point toward laurel trees.
Leather strapped onto your hips, due to your limits as a mortal,
And tanned before your destruction by magic.
You remember the creature you embroidered on your thigh.
How the inside of your thigh flickered with magic for days after his
arrival.
His body from what you're told.
Yep. So boring right now. Like you're staring at charcoal.
You can't really go hiding like this.
The Savior of the Multiverse then announced himself,
With all his pompous words. You can't be anywhere close.
You need to see or tell him how that feels.
You can't even look at him. He stares so pure, and perfect though he is.
You looked straight at his face because you need to talk.
You know he's just as confused about you as you think he is.
What you don't know though is how you're supposed to explain all
this to him.
And you follow him from the back seat, where you didn't feel much.
You guess you're afraid of being in the passenger seat, unable to help.
You turned your head to look back at him.
Kid manages to get dressed while you chat to you.
You recall the creature you embroidered on your thigh.

You want to ask him that now, but he can't hear you, or see you.
Is she messy.
You're warned. No, she's smart, and she's gonna integrate.
You're just gonna try and help her. Now what?
Your eyes wander back to the car door.
You wonder if your clothes are bleeding another bit themselves,
With the dirt that's in your hair.
You have a few more hours before they decide to neuter you,
Or use your scalp as a place to transport the bodies of the Grayson
farmers.
You're starting to suffer from depression from
The terrible act of breaking up with your husband and breaking up
with man.
The Job is as dull and dreary as you remembered.
You wind your way forward, trying to near the edge of the
Seemingly endless outer space
Of the space beyond normal.

Magic in Your Eyes

I am spreading magic
In the world that's out there.
Magic through the world that is growing
Cause now it's not only small stories.
Magic for one small thing
Will reach the whole world.
I am expanding my thoughts
For I see all of them.
I am spreading magic in the world that it is.
There is magic in your singing
When you sing to me and tell me to sing.
I am lighting the path to all magical things
So that all the little people can find.
There is magic in your eyes
When you are not listening to what I say
And watch the light in your ears wait.
And when you were afraid of the world
Magic came to you to tell me that it's worth
And you don't have to run away anymore.
There is magic in dusting your body
When the sand even crumbles to dust.
Like ice from the mountain when you trudge across the ground.
There is magic in your fingertips,
Magic with your light
And with your other hand that knows its way.
I know then that there is magic in me
I know that there is magic in your beauty
Must be that it makes you
Reach your full potential.
I want you to be free...

I want you to be free...
I want you to be free once again...
I want you to be free and to feel the endless magic.
And then I want you to grow old well,
Be safe, and wise,
As I am, I pray you grow old not yours mind.
I love you... I know you don't always hear me,
But I know that you still love me to be
The curves of my hands, collisions and my long braids Youths.
I love you.
I love you.

Incorrect Delivery

At first blush, the answer, my try, might seem incorrect,
Though I know the answers I give, would make you split,
When you're already conjuring about the wrong things.
"Poisoned,"□ said the man with the carnival grin,
"Are all the things you have been asked to pray.
It contained, holograms tell you the witnesses, town,
Venture company, kids, of a break-in botched at dawn,
A rescue from hell made of dreams,
Each thousand dark deep thoughts hidden by sunset.
Party eyes twitch, worms on their very skin,
Their body is just something they have turned into,
Each is a discovery of a lifetime.
"Poisoned,"□ the man laughs,□ □"You'll learn of someone . . . "□□
A rumor in town. No great peril, no limit to fear,
They knew, the whole town knew,
A river of blood in the corner,
Inside the walls of the sky,
And water on the ground, why was there?
I'll extend with grownups and kids,
In the shadows of youth,
Flames falling at midnight,
Flames sparking in the night sky . . .
Here in the control room,
I told you, □He smiled,□ □□□□□
This is the point of ignorance, my miss,
I know the riddle,□ □□but I need your control to make it go away.
□□
What you do, and say,
□This thing that took Command for big moment,□ □□□
□□□□□□□

□You rip your fingers away from your brains to rub,□ □□□
□□□□□□□
You laugh and giggle,□ □□□ □□□□
□Gently tap the fun board on your bare hand,
Don't let your friends see,
□Because here in that much honor,□ □□□ □□□□□□□
They'll see the flame lit torch silk wrapping,
And you'll see Big beaming at your back,
And all of the shadows, childhood.□□□
□"Poison,"□ I said. □"Poisoned,"□ said the man with the carnival
smile,□ □□□□□□□
"Have it," □I told them. □ □They had it all planned out,□
□□□they were ready. □□ □□□□□□□□□□
□The delivery took place in a lot of detail,□ □□□□
□□And the live stream was recorded with a cameraman,□ □□
□□The pain, the suffering,□ □□
□□(No names,□ □but fat two backs of thick leather satin)□
□□□□□
Hot and desiccated to the skin,□ □□
□□(There were not even a few records of symptoms,□ □□□□
Including worsening when Mrs. Murphy sighed
And said my guess,□ □□and then got it right). □□
□I wasn't surprised□ □we had heroes,□ □□□□□□□□
Because□, □they come in many flavors,□ □□□□□
But most of them remain strange.
I think nobody is as surprised as you should be,□ □□□
□□But why were you shocked?□□□□□
□As I sat there listening to all the grownups,□ □□□□□□
Singing innocent songs to children,□ □□
□□I listened to my own voice scratch like this,□ □□□□□
And the pendulum swung back and forth.□ □□□

I do not understand□ □how you can describe the□ □ shade,□
□□□□□

Not upscale the price ivory□ □□□
When the ban grandmother runs innocent jokes on our ashes.□ □
□□

Who art you to tell me I am not stirred with love
When the streets are overrun,□ □with sacrificial bunnies?□ □□□□
□Raised like sheep to fall at the feet of the gate?□ □capitals?□□

Ismael S. Rodriguez Jr. is a writer, poet, artist, and origami artist. He is originally from Philadelphia, PA but currently lives in Oakland Park, FL. He is a U.S. Navy veteran who served during Desert Storm. He is dual diagnosed with schizophrenia and a substance abuse problem and has experienced periods of homelessness. He now has 11 years clean and sober and is mentally and emotionally stable and in treatment for his issues. He is an ordained reverend and a Grey Witch who is also interested in Discordianism and ceremonial magick. He has a website where he posts poems, origami, and other things. The website is at https://thebulletproofpoet1.godaddysites.com/home that link as well as other links can be found at https://linktr.ee/bulletproofpoet.

9 798224 778676